I0162968

E.C.H.O.
Exhibition | Clarity | Healing | Oneness

By:

Marteena O.
&
Nakeia Danielle

ISBN-13:978-0692714942 (MNWritings)
ISBN-10:0692714944

Non Solum.

E.C.H.O.

We invite you on an exploration of our version of events, as two completely separate stories naturally intermingle and resound simultaneously as if they were fated to collide. This book was a labor of countless levels of love, and it is one of the greatest, most cleansing feelings in the world to share this journey with you. You... whoever and wherever you are... in your struggles, in your hopes, in your desires, in your crisis, in your happiness, in your dreams, in your laughter, in your uncertainty, in your aspirations, in your fears, in your joys, in your darkest moments...you are not alone. Thank you God for blessing my life with a channel, and a voice. Thank you to the many souls who have ignited my passion, my pain, my ability to free-fall without hesitation into the unknown. I am forever indebted, it is because of you that I am brave.

You gave me a *story*..

-Marteena O.

Writing introduces me to my soul. It's my safe place. I can be vulnerable. I can be raunchy. I can be ugly. I can be strong. I can be selfish. I am all of these things, intricately intertwined with rag and bone. The journey is contradictory. Hindsight visits way more often than insight. Nothing ever makes sense. Limbo becomes an all too familiar acquaintance. Night seems darker, longer. Nonetheless, I've discovered that through all the blood, sweat, tears, seminal, and vaginal fluids, out arises growth. None come out unscathed, yet the journey is flawless. This is its echo.

With Love,
Nakeia Danielle

THE JOURNEY

Exhibition.

ex·hi·bi·tion (n) -an event at which objects **(such as works of art)** are put out in a public space for people to look at.

[I lowered my aura an octave
& all that became audible

were the wars]
the world was *braving...*

-Reverberate

E.C.H.O.

You called me, and I came running. Add that to the list
of times...

[I didn't *listen*.]

Dumb as I seem, numb as I pretend to be,
energies radiate, and obliterate our past,
Every wrong becomes *undone*.
Completely enamored, you are *allure*.
Your scent is native to my senses,
I know when you are near.

I tussle with my feelings as they
twine like vines entangling a wall.

I surrender,
I succumb,
you win, you've won,

like you've *always* done...

-Stubborn

Residue

Romanticized my affliction
Pacified an addiction
to feeling needed, wanted
by you.
Kept you close enough to hope for a forever
yet far enough to sever an affinity I never outgrew.
You lied, you fronted
on me.
Introduced me to misery.
I missed every sign, ignored every cue.
Running back, always running,
running back to you.
Forgive me of my ignorance.
If you could have witnessed it,
in my innocence,
dysfunction was the only love I knew.

WWIII
Teach me your secrets...

How do you make letting go look so seamless?
How do I prevent the sorrow of missing you?

Teach me not to be broken by your inability to love me
How do I accept your nonchalance?
I shared with you every ounce of my soul
The same soul once protected by A-K's
and bulletproof vest
Until I laid eyes on you, I no longer felt at war
Or maybe I no longer feared the risk of casualty
And these are the end results.

Me Too
I try to ignore that I desire nothing more than for you to
miss me too
Like somehow knowing
I cross your mind
would ease the process
I hope somewhere you are trying to ignore your
feelings, but losing the battle
to the overwhelming power of truth
I hope somewhere you're paddling frantically
to stay above water, yet maintaining a forced smile
Nonetheless,
I'm learning to miss you

Just please miss me too.

You appeared, in the
midst of the monotony that was me.
Day in, day out, same lyrics on loop, same melody.
There you were, a rhythm that
I couldn't read from ear.
I wished that I could keep you,
but your bustling brevity
would soon devour the excitement,
the enticement,
evanescently you'd disappear.
With you I saw the **vividness** of life.
Blue became *cerulean*,
and love began to bloom again in my garden.
And when I press my cheek to other beats, no other
sound is as satisfying, nor as sweet.
Low fidelity,
I guess I will spend an eternity settling for samples, of
your one-man symphony.
I'm filled with the feeling that
you'll be booming in my memory,
for moons that don't yet know they glow...

I guess this is how *soulmates* flow.

-Interlude

E.C.H.O.

What makes the unavailable so alluring?
Do you not feel deserving of reciprocation?
Does it hurt your ego to accept rejection?
Is acceptance the true problem?
When will you love yourself enough not to
tolerate anything less than your worth?
Do you feel fulfilled chasing pavements?
What is your worth?

Questions for Women Like Me

Wanted
I wonder what a wonder it is, being witlessly admired
Having gentlemen inquire, whisper, conspire:
"Who's that queen?"
Walk mean
Talk mean
Intellectual fiend
By one, by many
Do I devalue as they divvy?
I ask, cause I'm not privy
to the fortunes of
the *pretty*.

RED
The perfect pop of color,
smothered in her ambiance,
heads turned as she burned through every room.
A smile cut like diamonds,
Piercing gaze, mental maze,
articulate and well-behaved.
Like a fever climbing,
she infiltrated you.
A bawse, a queen, a poet
the way tailored garments
romanticized her outlines.
In all her glamour, she remained undefined by time.
You were not phased by any other.
She was the lady in red, and I am her daughter.

Repressed
I can't even begin to decipher all the cryptic messages
locked in my heart
I don't know how to feel
What's hidden behind
these coded memories
I'm numb to the pain of my existence
Numb to the lack of relationship I have with the woman
whose womb nurtured my growth
Numb to the man who abandoned me, yet he is
present every day
I look in the mirror
I don't know how to express
Evading made me feel free,
until it enslaved me
Ignorant to how all these
things shaped me
Needy, introverted, distrusting, self-centered
Lost in the world
Opening Pandora's box

Facing all the feelings repressed.

E.C.H.O.

Daddy's Girl

I look in the mirror and see your face
Empty memories that time cannot erase
I don't know how to deny you
Everything in me has remnants of you
I would say I don't need you
Then I think of how you could have coached me to avoid so much
of life's strife
How you could have taught me to avoid the mistreatment of
careless men
Daddy never reiterated my beauty
Sometimes I hate you, and I'm glad I've thrived without you
Today my soul needs you, and accepts that that will always reign
true.

Brown Girl

Brown girl,
you are beauty from the flexors in your feet, to the laugh lines
surrounding your cheeks, through the thickness in your thighs,
legacy in your eyes
Brown girl
you are the daughter of Rosa, Nefertiti, Madame CJ, Sheba,
Cleopatra, Mrs. King,
Brown girl
you are a fighter, the cradle of life, queen, supreme being,
Brown girl
you are a God fearing masterpiece, your mind supersedes all that
is limiting
Brown girl
you are not your daddy issues, not the remnants of a boy who left
you peace-less, in pieces
Brown girl
If he loves you, he will learn you, if he earns you he will yearn you, if
you inspire him, he will lead, if he dims your light,
let him leave
Brown girl
you are not entangled in the psychological noose society hangs
above your head, you are **free**,
to believe to dream to be
Brown girl
You are infinity
Brown Girl
You are me.

I AM

I am
The woman who knows she is loved without the constant desire for affirmation
The woman who knows she is missed even when his pride won't admit it
I am every woman
Dripping in gold from head to toe
My love overflows easily
It liberates because it is unconstrained
Confident in my beauty because my flaws are hand-crafted divinity
Not merely complementary, but necessary
Never questioning my greatness
Anyone ignorant will be enlightened by ethereal energy
I am woman
I am the universe
I am purity
I am strength
I am love
I am blessings
I am energy
I am attempting to claim this.

[Of my being, my blackness was the first thing I earned] and the last thing I accepted.

-Birthright

Black Like Me
Where can I be black
Everywhere I turn I'm under attack
Where can I pray
Where do I find solace,
hope that everything will be okay
Where can I drive
Where can I thrive
Where can I walk
Where can I talk
Where can I feel
Where can I heal
It is so hopeless being black like me
Proud, heavy-hearted, overwhelmed, enraged
Always searching for a way out of this cage
Fighting for existence
Incessantly rout with resistance
Where can I be free
When will it be okay to be black like me?

Strangers

Same city, different worlds.
Same culture, different thrills.
Same streets, different schools.
Different genders, different rules.
Same struggle, different hustle.
Same government, same bubble.
Same stigmas, different views.
Same disdain for the boys in blue.
Same roots, different pigment.
Some ebony, some light skin-ded.
Same summers, different winters.
My sister, my brother, my father, my mother.
I know you, you know me.
The same saints, different sinners.
Bound by history, estranged by the mystery
of where we are going.
Strangers.

Freedom is my religion
Freedom is my slavery
Drowning in the abyss
Dreaming of when these
unshed tears will turn into bliss

-Freedom

One of the boys

Went to school on your game,
learned the trade, get in get out,
cue memory fade,
of who you could have been to me.
Emotional unavailability, masked fragility.
Can I cuff and then bluff?
Can I lust and ruin trust?
I wanna see you bleed.

Can I?
Be the lioness instead of the gazelle?
Look you in your eyes, put you under a spell?
Meet you on Monday forget to call you on Sunday,
send a text, a year later wishing you well?

Let me.
Leave you in need.
Make you another conquest, sign you up for this
contest, for a heart not longing to be captured.

Can I?
Make you question your beauty,
leave you confused, egotistically bruised,
used, accused of forgetting the arrangement to remain
nameless and avoid being enraptured?

But this is a boy's game in man's world,
and a man's woman is always once a boy's girl.
You may forget my name, but karma traces faces.

No worthy lessons in trading spaces.

ART & NUMBERS
For him, everything needed a reason
For her, everything needed a rhythm.
She was on a frequency somewhere between
restlessness and tranquility,
In her he found peace.

He was art,
in the way that gravity cradled his enormity.
In him she found adventure.

Their auras collided,
energies coincided.
A bond so enigmatic, organic,
native to another planet.

A calculated abstraction from the very start.
For her, he was numbers
For him, she was art.

Cocoon
I am going on this inward journey.
When I resurface on kaleidoscope wings,
Your eyes, your soul, and your aura are the
first things I hope to set on *fire*. . .

Biochemical Lover
You penetrate all my thoughts
Jumping from synapse to synapse
Backfiring bliss and sadness
Full and empty
Everything and nothing
Rich and poor
Too much and never enough.

It was a moth to the flame kind of thing. I,
the pretty specimen, you were to blame
for the inferno dancing in my eyes.
I fell in love.
Infatuated with the simplicity in your stride,
how you seemed so careless in the thick of the chaos
that was our youth.
I realized I couldn't keep you the
moment you smiled.
You belonged to everyone, and no one.
The utmost unattainable, yet the only thing worth
calling mine.
If the stars were aligned,
there was nothing to complicate, nothing to
contemplate,
nothing will ever outweigh or equate
the gravity of you and I.
-Moth to the Flame

Masterpiece
Just me, you, and your bedroom eyes
laying on top of the world
staring at a starry night
painted by either Van Gogh or God.
I can't quite recall,
but it's odd,
I remember
how endlessly I fall
for you,
over and over, a thousand times, and
always once more.

E.C.H.O.

In his presence I was cocooned,
afraid to be consumed by
the wildfire raging between us.

But he laid gentle eyes and hands
within my atmosphere,
whispered softly in my ear:

*"Lay your burdens down, next to your crown, and make
love to me."*

-Vulnerable

Sex Haze
I want to feel the grasp of man
Hands caressing every
God designed curve of my body
Top to bottom
Front to back
Pull my hair as you fill me from behind
I want to inhale every inch
Fuck moaning
I want to lose my breath
Spread my lips and revive me
Over and under
I'll fulfill your every desire
Again, and again, and again.

Love letters (wishful thinking)

 In your love letters,

You feed me Plato, Aristotle, Hip-Hop, Gangsta Rap
idealism, Greek gods, Orion's Belt, gender gap
Parisian romance, Venice nights,
Black American legends,
the game of chess,
my rook, at your knight
You feed me other, you feed me art.

These things lay densely on my mental for days,
that's food for thought.
So I wrote you a *love letter*,
About the way we **vibrate**,
as we hold hands and glimpse at sunsets too
divine not to encounter.
There are waves and more world beyond us,
clouds kiss the rebellious skies above us,
I'm hoping it won't grow dark and cold too soon,
kind of like how I feel towards you.

Cause I want to write you so many love letters,
But since I know better, about forever…

It may be best to exist in "the *gray*",
if it means a chance for another 'today'

                              and another *love letter*.

Philly
I sat up one night on what felt like the edge of a cliff
and wondered if you've spent your summers since...

with another girl sitting shotgun in
your cherry red sedan 'til 2 a.m.
as you two ponder life together.
My eyes become waterfalls at the thought of you
dwelling in that
sweet simplicity with someone else.

Was I so easy to replace?
Have you forgotten my face,
and how the city tastes when you kiss me?
You are king in my memory.

Los Angeles
I'll think of you more than I'll admit is true,
I'll miss you more than I know how to do.

[I keep adding
brushstrokes of hues to this
pretty picture in hopes that my]

varied syntax eventually *moves* you...

-1,000 words

The Artisan/The Muse

He looked at me with galaxies in his eyes.
Studied my body's language.
He knew me forever, and I still took him by surprise.

Every meeting was a blank canvas.

He used his finest brushes to paint a million smiles
on replicas of an elegant visage,
but none were as pristine, none were spitting image.

None quite like his muse.

He traced and outlined my mind, valued my opinion.
Memorized my dimensions, soothed my afflictions.
Cared for me like one of his mediums.
Polished, properly placed, and put away to safety.

He couldn't replace me.

I danced gracefully by his side to the music he
composed.
But soon, inspiration ran cold,
We grew compromised
Knowing I belonged to him,
 while his heart belonged to another.

I was merely his muse.

He, an eternal, *almost* **lover**.

A Love Deferred (Ode to Langston Hughes)

What happens to a love deferred?
Does it fade away
Like night into day
Or blossom like flowers in May
And then shrivel up
Does it feel fatal?
Or does it renew and restore
Like prayer on Sunday morning
Maybe it just changes form
Like H2O
Or does it just disappear?

Love Stories
I want to write love stories
Tales of hearts so intertwined it's impossible to fathom
how they ever beat separately
Reinforce that love is available to all
That we all have a universe designed celestial body
awaiting our solar return
Then I get distracted by you.

Hues
Sometimes my sunny yellow,
can't permeate your cloudy gray.
Indigo is where you go when literature leaves your lips
to kiss my frontal lobe.
Maroon is how passionate the passion gets when we
reach the bed flaming red.
Money green, is your favorite,
you'd paint the city if you could.
Plume purple is mine, I prefer power, I'm the queen
other girls never could
Be. to. you.
And I'm tickled pink, when you trace your fingertips
along my laugh lines.
Crimson red around my head when people wonder in
awe about our aims.
Melted milky way brown down to tiny honey tones, is
what happens when we lay *mixed*, richness to a T.
Still, I'm blinded by the jet black of your aura in those
moments when you are not easy to read.
Winter white is what it sounds like when space grows
between our colors.
Eliminate my yellow if I can't have my blue.

Through every shade, love never fades,
you are my favorite hue.

Luxury
I don't need no first class flights,
to these fancy suites,
on those pink beaches where
summer never sleeps.
They say where you feel alive,
where you feel at peace,
where you're one with nature is
where you're **complete**.

In fact,

spending Saturdays with my head in your lap, while we
recite lyrics from
our favorite raps will always be

the greatest *luxury*.

Sand between tinged toes
Flowers round my crown
sun kissed melanin
Ocean breezes dampening my tresses
This is where my mind is *24/7*

Who says you can't always live life, like you're on
vacation?

-Mindstate

Clarity.

clar·i·ty (n): the quality of being certain or definite; the quality of transparency or purity.

[Clarity] is often times better than closure.

-Epiphanic

Finally Free
I rather love you than hate you
Pretending that you aren't celestial is hard work
So I accept reality
Even if it's not with me
Your beauty is far beyond what eyes can see
My desire for you is more profound than the desert's
desire for sea
It's unhealthy for me not to love you
So I'll love you now and forever
I hope that is freeing to you
Because finally it freed me too.

Alchemy
I will succumb to the pain of change if it means
becoming a better "me" means
being ready,

 for a better "you."

Hunter

She was this elusive, nimble creature,
that lived in the winds...

No matter how wild and ravenous his pursuit grew,

Her evanescence challenged him

He struggled in the awareness of being

Unable to *captivate* her...

[Now I understand that,
Sometimes words are just words...

Even those coveted]

'I love you's'...

-Empty

Clarity
The universe knew we weren't in the stars
You and I separately will bear the scars
To understand is to love
To love is to free.
Sometimes clarity is bliss
Sometimes clarity is pain
And the search for it all will drive you insane.

Distance and Time
It takes no time.
Nostalgia fills the mental space, where I keep you.
Me time is we time, and if I get to see time go by
it served as an inconvenience.

You echoed in the Arizona canyons,
I lusted for you in the hot Nevada suns,
dreamt of you in the Carolinas,
where the Atlantic engulfs solemn sands,
aiming tirelessly to be one.
Kind of like me for you, and...

Recollection of your facial features is my favorite
pastime, you still send chills up my spine,
as I wonder if I lay phantom to your left every night,
my pillow clenched to my chest so tight, in an attempt
to feel you.

Or do you fill my space with half hearts, in hopes that I'll
come home, one day to say, "I always knew you were
the one..."

All it took was distance and time.

The Undoing
The moment you told me you didn't like poetry
Love died, intertwining unraveled.
look at all the pretty words you made hug these empty
pages.

You could not fathom the very thing
you inspired within me,
the very thing that made "us",

but "we"
were actors on stages.

The irony of it all
we were going nowhere,

when we hit a **wall**...

Boredom
Even though it makes me blue
Missing you gives me something to do...

*Losing you was **worth** living this enormous...*

-On road

Juxtaposition
I'm passive
I'm aggressive
I'm quiet
I'm loud
I'm love
I'm indifference
I'm normal
I'm insane
I'm open and closed

Paradox
I'm the most selfless when I'm selfish
I can be arrogant, because I've been humbled
I risked the trip, so I'm permitted to stumble
I'm an angel at times, but this angel has demons
Sometimes I lose sight of what I believe in
White-collar artist/poetess/peaceful-political
Hunger is familiar because I work to stay full
A tainted virgin, educated domestic,
an ugly kind of beautiful
Fearful of a four cornered excursion
Cosmopolitan one day, provincial the next
To some I'm in first place, to others
I'm tired, tarnished,
I'm second best
Often I'm the teacher, mostly still a student
But All the time am I **human**, however flawed,
however in-congruent.

The Princess of Ruin

I make promises I know I'll never keep
I say poetic things I know I don't mean
I'm lonely
Always searching for fulfillment
If you come around now I might use you
Try to twist and bend you into something I want
When I realize you don't fit I'll throw you away
So just run away
I never recognize my ability to destroy until I'm
surrounded by debris
I can't be everything to you until I'm everything to me
I have to map my way out of lonely.

Dear Lonely,
We have to learn to coexist
Our encounters can't always be so catastrophic
Old lovers aren't cures
Drugs aren't band-aids
Lies aren't magic potions
I have to accept your place in my heart
Grow in your wisdom
Find creativity in your stupor
Comfort in your silence.

XY Issues
I don't know how to love
I think it's your fault
Your presence reminds me of my first heartbreak.

Some people make art,
some people *are* art.

_Matter

My Generation

How have we become masters of empty intimacy?
How do we pour love in and over each other and then
feel nothing?
How are we so deep, yet vastly shallow?
Consumed with fake pleasures and lonely nights.
Great pretenders.
Too proud to really feel.
Where did we learn these things?
When did we discover how to be so full of nothing?

"22"
We were **lost.**
Our only homes were in each other's hearts.
We owned the nights, day light was too residual of reality:
They convinced us we were only candles in the sun.

Post grad, most had nothing.
But we got high, paycheck to paycheck we got by,
relentless soul searching was the mission,
our eyes saw farther than most, but fear clouded the vision,
Fail or fly, do or die, this was the moment.

We danced in and out of lust, *trust was evanescent,*
We made a mess of love in search of the definition
of true intimacy, a soul tie that would outgrow time.

Unsatisfied with existing, we needed to
feel alive, to live vivid,
cause we were worth winning
everything.

All we held on to was **hope.**
our talent was enough,
our intellect was enough,
our cosmopolitan thoughts,
forgiveness for the youth in our faults...
Faith in God, faith in ourselves, faith in the universe..
It was enough to get us where we were going..

Now we know there's nothing missing.
These words were worth venting,
In case you felt this way too..

at 22.

The perks of being a Wilde Flower

Young and restless, young and reckless
This is how we live:
Ruled by nature
Blooming demi-gods
Children of beyond
Wanderers
Interpreters of space
Critics of time
We believe in the movies
We believe in lyrics
Children of the sky
Millennial hippies
Free spirits
Deranged butterflies with
Glowing coronas
Sunflowers dancing in summer rain
Honey Bees that sting
With **passion**
Sweet nectars drip from our lips
Salt and vinegar drained from our veins
Princesses of poets
Classic, always in fashion
Curators of love stories
Students of aesthetics
Humbled by our glory
We know the secret.

Reality is nothing as it seems.

So we *live in our dreams*.

Never No More

[I'm addicted to the allure
The mystery behind eyes concealing more
I always think I'm the door

Never no more...]

Healing.

heal·ing (n): the process of making or becoming sound or healthy again.

I Wish I Could Cry

I wish I could cry away my sadness
With every tear release my misunderstood anguish
I wish I could cry my way to love
With each tear release all my feelings of inadequacy
and self-loathing
I wish I could cry a river of loss
With each tear leading toward a sea of glee
I wanna cry for my mother
I wanna cry for my father
I wanna cry for my sister and brothers
I wanna cry for all the generations who never shed
tears in fear of weakness
My tears will drown away all the sorrows of yesterday
My tears will hydrate a wealth of new life tomorrow
I wish I could cry.

E.C.H.O.

You Let Me Fall
You're innocent
I came in like a thief in the night
Aiming to steal your heart
But you're clever
You had it locked away, you knew I would come looking
I was persistent, I thought maybe I could figure out your combination
You'd turn the dial and stop right before anything was revealed
But you let me in your space
Showed me how to get to the safe
I could hear your heart beating behind the lock
Then you kicked me out.

She'll never believe me
If I told her I wasn't ready...
Ready for a forever, when frankly I only have today.
She deciphered that I entice her, with no real intentions to stay.
Hate to make her think she's an afterthought, when all I envision is that she's a vision in white.
Her insecurities are fallacies, men of their word are an **anomaly**.
I'm either the wind beneath her wings, or the rain hindering her flight.
This thing is fated, I'm hoping.
She's speeding, I'm coasting.
My love, rivers flow into oceans.
I can paint the bigger picture, but I can't make her see.
Sometimes tiny details tend to breed deceit.

So we remain a mystery, from my

-POV

Denial
I've been neglecting my heart
Ignoring the way it skips at the sight of your face
All this emotional shit is **overwhelming**
So I'll spend my nights thinking of you
I'll close my eyes and dream of you
And when I wake, I'll *neglect my heart*.

Truth
I'm afraid I'm falling for an angel
My heart has made you too perfect
That's what's scary
The thought of not seeing a real person, but an ideal
I find beauty in the things I don't like about you
Opening myself so wide that shit loads of hurt could
enter, and take too long to leave.

You can't keep falling **apart** . . .

-Citadel

E.C.H.O.

Object of My Desire
The thoughts that terrorize your mind nightly
Let me love them to a place of no return
The ugly you hide from the world
I'll reveal its bizarre, **eccentric beauty**
I'm not afraid of *walls*
I'll show you the rubble from where mine fell down
Bring me your dark, I'll transform it into *sun-rays*.

Echoes of Silence
My lessons are silent
They creep into your subconscious and
become your improved mentality
If you are still enough you'll become aware
Aware of my wisdom in your thoughts
My *gentleness* in your words
My lessons are free
They deposit into your spirit
and become your improved existence
You'll see strength where there once was weakness
Weakness I softly nurtured into **Kingdom**
So silently you missed me.

Relocation
Ghosts of who and what we were hover all over this town.
I tried hard to stay down. You worked hard at giving up.
Too much of me and you not enough of **"us"**.
I made a home out of you, everybody knew my address.
And now I don't know you, like *I knew you.*
Moving out and **moving on**.

I wanna go where nobody knows my love..

Au Naturel
Completely naked, in the raw
no man made legislation.
only the laws written by nature rule.
Time spent is sublime.
Fingering through blank pages
unknowingly bound to my story.
No more forcing squares into circles.
You opened my eyes to my true definition,
accurate dimensions.
I must mention. . .
Beware of the rough edges, I've been known to leave
scars.
But as long as you're brave, I will be bare.
Share my world.
As it will be, As it is, as it was...

I sat beside myself one day in an attempt to introduce
myself to me:

who was I?
who am I?
and who in lieu of the latter
was I going to be?

-Grasshopper

"The *universe* will not come to you unless you are **still**.

It is just as intimidated by
your *imbalance* as you are
by its **heaviness**

It must sense,
trust the readiness for the **abundance**
you have been *marked* for.
Submit to the oneness your (trinity) mind, body, and
soul seeks,

and everything will be *poured into you.* "

-Sensei

Oneness.

one ·ness (n) : the quality or state or fact of being one;
wholeness.

[Imagine if we called each and every imperfection]
a *beauty mark*.

-Beauty Marks

[I figured at 23 my quest to be the most beautiful version of myself should go deeper than what I could exhibit physically, what I could post on a social medium, or what I could convince another I was confident of...]

-Inner Beauty

"Time alone with my gift, is time alone with my God."

-Meditation

"Faith and Fear cannot coexist."

-Affirmed

- -

We are all...

Coming to terms with the fact that **life will break you**, but also that you must find something to cling to, to remind you of what it is to be whole.

Yes, I guess that's when most creatives stumble upon their true artistry—when they begin

to master their pieces. . .

Thrifty
I refuse to accept your second-hand emptiness
It's foreign and uncomfortable
I can't handle your empty
I've copyrighted my own empty
For me, by me
My empty is liberating
My empty is free
My emptiness is curated by me.

Summer
Love is one of life's greatest mysteries.
There are no theorems or philosophical findings
worthy of defining what's happening here tonight,
between you and I.
So let's not calculate the give and take, the reciprocity
or our mistakes, if we're not ready time will wait, and in
this moment our hearts will stay.
So just hold me.

Tides

I want to be synonymous with the ocean.
Uncontainable, Unpredictable, Unfathomable
And I'll only ever dance for my *lover*, the moon.

E.C.H.O.

There's an ocean within,
can you *swim*?

-Fathom

Sink or Swim
They say I'm too deep
That sometimes I should dumb it down and only release
my passion in doses
I guess a mere hit of my energy is intoxicating
I guess mortals OD when my soul enters the ear and
penetrates the cerebral cortex
And maybe it's sobering to blame it on my deepness.

I can't wait
to meet you and know that I knew you in another life.
To love you infinitely, differently every day.
To be confident, that God graced my existence to be
from, of, and by your side.
-Rib

Beautiful Stranger
I know you
I feel your embrace with the passing of the wind
I care for you
I feel your fears and soul aches, your passions and
inspirations
I love you
I feel your faith penetrating my emotions,
voice rewiring my circuitry
I need you
I feel your aura filling my lungs, your wisdom running
through my veins
Yet, I have never met you.

Rain
When it pours I think of you
Your beauty
Your havoc
Your necessity
Your inability to be controlled or contained
I think of life when I see you
I daydream of your existence
Of the day I get to hold you in my arms
We'll already be familiar because I have been caught
in your rapture numerous times
I'll tell you of the love I had for you before we met
I'll share with you all the reasons why
As we walk in the *rain.*

The earth is
burning,
sinking,
receding,
cracking,
turning itself upward. . .

[**But** your fingers are warm, and intertwined with mine.]

-**Haven**

Love is Stronger Than Pride
I don't remember what it is like to be in your arms
To feel you inside my pink matter
Feels like a distant memory
I still hold you in my dreams
You love me in my subconscious
In reality I still miss you
I still wish I could lie on your chest
Listening to the synchronizing of our heartbeats
You have probably forgotten these moments
They are forever etched in my soul
You were my metaphysical first
You were innate to my spirit
You unveiled what no other man could
Your absence taught me more than your presence
ever would.
Love is stronger than pride.

E.C.H.O.

Vibrate Higher
My spirit vibrates to levels I cannot fathom
Desires places that do not exist.
Feels emotions attached to no reality
My soul runs deep
So deep it doesn't understand its beauty in a world
consumed with the depths of shallow waters.

\- \- \-

Radiate
My darling,
The world is big and cold.
Though darkness will implore you
In many moments,
You must work your hardest to
Always exist
In the light.

To possess both a story and a voice, is to hold an *obligation* to the **universe**.

-Angels

End;
Sometimes I have to remind myself
that I too am just
rag and bone
and that my ultimate accomplishment will be,

growing content with returning to **dust**.

Interlude
Never cling so tightly to the destination that you miss
the journey.

This moment is all that exists. . .

www.ingramcontent.com/pod-product-compliance
Lightning Source LLC
Chambersburg PA
CBHW060039050426
42448CB00012B/3081